Irish Stews

Irish Stews

Aisling O'Connor

illustrated by

Andrew Selby

HAMLYN

897643

ACKNOWLEDGEMENTS

Art Director Jacqui Small

Designer Louise Leffler

Executive Editor Susan Haynes

Editor Kathy Steer

Production Controller Melanie Frantz

Illustrator Andrew Selby

First published in 1995 by Hamlyn
an imprint of Reed Consumer Books Limited
Michelin House, 81 Fulham Road, London SW3 6RB
and Auckland, Melbourne, Singapore and Toronto.

ISBN 0 600 58580 8
A CIP catalogue record for this book is available at the British Library.
Printed in Hong Kong

NOTES

Both metric and imperial measurements have been given in all recipes.
Use one set of measurements only and not a mixture of both.
Standard level spoon measurements are used in all recipes.
1 tablespoon = one 15 ml spoon   1 teaspoon = one 5 ml spoon
Eggs should be size 3 and milk full fat unless otherwise stated.
Ovens should be preheated to the specified temperature – if using a fan
assisted oven, follow the manufacturer's instructions for adjusting
the time and the temperature.

Contents

Introduction

Irish Stew is Ireland's version of the traditional peasant one-pot stew. In Ireland, as in other European countries, small cottages did not have ovens. They did, however, have open fires, used for heating and cooking. The stew would cook, hanging from a brazier over the fire, or on the hearth before it. This cooking method is long and slow - perfectly suited to the cheaper, tastier cuts of meat used for this dish. The final texture should not be thin like soup, but rich, thick and filling.

Traditionally it is said, mutton or kid was used for Irish Stew. But nowadays, it is most often made with lamb, and we have used neck or shoulder chops, or stewing lamb in our recipes. You will also find dishes with beef, pork and chicken. Even one used by cooks in East Africa which includes milk, and others for more splendid occasions which include wine or stout.

The essential ingredient, however, is the potato - introduced to Ireland in the late 1500s by Sir Walter Raleigh, by the middle of the 18th Century it was the staple food for Irish families.

Traditional Irish Stew

500 G/1 LB FLOURY POTATOES, PEELED AND SLICED

500 G/1 LB ONIONS, PEELED AND SLICED

1 KG/2 LBS LAMB CHOPS

300 ML/½ PINT WATER

12 SMALL NEW POTATOES, PEELED

12 SMALL ONIONS, PEELED

SALT AND FRESHLY GROUND BLACK PEPPER

CHOPPED PARSLEY, TO GARNISH

1 Place half the floury potatoes and onions in a large deep saucepan and season with plenty of salt and pepper.

2 Add the chops and season well with salt and pepper. Place the remainder of the potatoes and onions on top and add more seasoning. Add water to just cover the meat and the vegetables and bring to the boil. Cover with a lid and cook slowly for 1 hour.

3 Remove the pan from the heat and add the new potatoes and small onions. If the stew is too thick add some more water, it should not be too thin. Return to the heat and cook for 1 hour.

4 Serve hot in bowls, garnished with chopped parsley.

Serves 4

Gaelic Stew

500 G/1 LB MIDDLE NECK OF LAMB

250 G/8 OZ POTATOES, SLICED

1 ONION, SLICED

2 CARROTS, SLICED

1 CELERY STICK, CHOPPED

½ TEASPOON DRIED MIXED HERBS

200 ML/⅓ PINT STOCK

15 G/½ OZ BUTTER, MELTED

SALT AND FRESHLY GROUND BLACK PEPPER

1 Divide the lamb into cutlets.

2 Cover the base of a 1.2 litre/2 pint casserole dish with half the potatoes. Arrange the lamb on top and sprinkle liberally with salt and pepper.

3 Mix together the onions, carrots, celery and herbs, with salt and pepper to taste. Spread over the lamb and pour over the stock. Arrange the remaining potatoes in overlapping circles on the top and brush with melted butter.

4 Cover the dish and cook in a preheated oven at 180°C (350°F) Gas Mark 4 for 1½ hours. Remove the lid and continue to cook for about 20 to 30 minutes until the potatoes are browned.

Serves 4

Irish Hot Pot

750 G/1½ LB UNSMOKED SLIPPER JOINT OF BACON, RIND REMOVED,
TRIMMED AND CUT INTO 2.5 CM/1 INCH CUBES
3 MEDIUM ONIONS, THINLY SLICED
5 CARROTS, SLICED
2 STICKS CELERY, SLICED
750 G/1½ LB LARGE POTATOES, THICKLY SLICED
LIGHT HAM-FLAVOURED OR VEGETABLE STOCK, TO COVER
15 G/½ OZ BUTTER, MELTED
SALT AND FRESHLY GROUND BLACK PEPPER

1 Place the bacon in a pan and cover with water. Bring slowly to the
boil, then drain well. Mix the onions, carrots, celery and
season with salt and pepper.

2 Put a layer of potatoes into a deep casserole dish, cover with a layer
of bacon and then with vegetables. Continue making layers, ending
with potatoes, then pour in the stock.

3 Cover the casserole and cook in a preheated oven at
170°C (325°F) Gas Mark 3 for 1½ hours.

4 Uncover and brush the potatoes with melted butter. Continue
cooking uncovered, until the stock has reduced and the potatoes are
tender. Serve the stew with fresh vegetables.

Serves 4

Irish Style Lamb Chops

50 G/2 OZ BUTTER

8 LAMB CHOPS

1 LARGE ONION, CHOPPED

1 TABLESPOON PLAIN FLOUR

1 x 411 G/14½ OZ CAN CONSOMMÉ

1 BOUQUET GARNI

1 KG/2 LB POTATOES, CUT INTO 4 CM/1½ INCH CHUNKS

SALT AND FRESHLY GROUND BLACK PEPPER

CHOPPED PARSLEY, TO GARNISH

1 Melt the butter in a large flameproof casserole. Add the lamb chops and brown on both sides, then remove and set aside. Add the onion to the casserole and fry until softened. Sprinkle over the flour and stir well, then return the chops to the casserole.

2 Pour over the consommé and add the bouquet garni with salt and pepper to taste. Bring to the boil, then cover and cook in a preheated oven at 180°C (350°F) Gas Mark 4 for about 1 hour.

3 Stir in the potatoes, re-cover the casserole and continue cooking for 45 minutes or until the chops are cooked and the potatoes are tender.

4 Remove the bouquet garni and garnish with parsley before serving.

Serves 4

Pot Roast Lamb with Vegetables

1 TABLESPOON SUNFLOWER OIL
1.75 KG/3½ LB LEG OF LAMB, CUT INTO BITE-SIZE PIECES
250 G/8 OZ LEEKS, SLICED THICKLY
375 G/12 OZ BABY TURNIPS
2 TABLESPOONS TOMATO PURÉE
1 BOUQUET GARNI
125 ML/4 FL OZ LAMB OR BEEF STOCK
SALT AND FRESHLY GROUND BLACK PEPPER

1 Heat the oil in a large pan and fry the lamb pieces to seal it on all sides. Remove the lamb and place it in a large, ovenproof casserole dish.

2 Add the vegetables to the pan and fry them quickly until they are lightly browned. Drain them well and arrange them around the lamb in the casserole. Add the tomato puree, bouquet garni, salt and pepper and pour over the stock.

3 Cover the casserole tightly and cook in a preheated oven at 160°C (325°F) Gas Mark 3 for about 2½ hours or until the lamb is tender. Discard the bouquet garni.

4 Carefully transfer the lamb to a warmed serving dish. Lift out the vegetables, draining them well, and arrange them around the meat. Skim off any fat from the juices and serve them separately in a gravy boat.

Serves 4

New Season Irish Stew

500 g/1 lb lean lamb, cut into pieces

1 tablespoon vegetable oil

2 medium onions, chopped

2 medium carrots, chopped

2 sticks celery, chopped

½ small swede, chopped

1 tablespoon flour

600 ml/1 pint stock

3 tomatoes, skinned and quartered

2 medium leeks, thinly sliced

150 ml/¼ pint red wine

500 g/1 lb new potatoes

salt and pepper

1 Place the lamb and oil in a casserole with the onions and carrots.
Fry for 5 minutes, then add the celery and swede and cook
until the meat is browned. Season to taste.

2 Remove from the heat and mix in the flour. Add the stock and
return to the heat, adding the tomatoes and leeks. Simmer for
15 minutes. Stir in the wine, cover and cook in a preheated oven
180°C (350°F) Gas Mark 4 for 30 minutes.

3 Boil the potatoes until almost cooked. Remove the casserole from
the oven, place potatoes on top and return uncovered to the oven for a
further 20-30 minutes. Serve immediately.

Serves 4

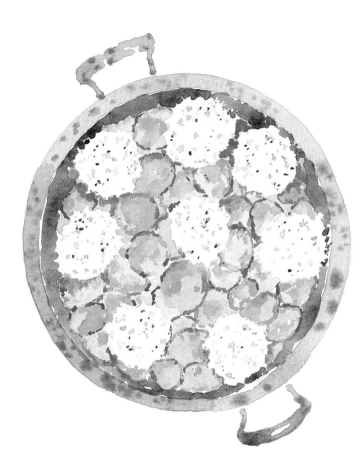

Irish Stew with Parsley Dumplings

1 KG/2 LB MIDDLE OR SCRAG END OF NECK LAMB CHOPS

3 LARGE ONIONS, SLICED

1 KG/2 LB POTATOES, SLICED

2 TABLESPOONS WORCESTERSHIRE SAUCE

FOR THE DUMPLINGS:

50 G/2 OZ SELF-RAISING FLOUR

50 G/2 OZ SOFT WHITE BREADCRUMBS

2 TABLESPOONS SHREDDED SUET

4 TABLESPOONS FRESHLY CHOPPED PARSLEY

1 EGG, BEATEN

SALT AND FRESHLY GROUND BLACK PEPPER

1 Arrange a layer of chops in a casserole and season to taste.
Cover with a layer of onions and then potatoes.
Repeat until all the onions and potatoes have been used.
2 Sprinkle the Worcestershire sauce over the top, pour in enough
water to come almost to the top. Cover and cook in a preheated oven
at 160°C (325°F) Gas Mark 3 for 2½ hours.
3 Make the dumplings by mixing the flour, breadcrumbs, suet, parsley
and seasoning in a bowl. Make a well in the centre and place the egg
in the well. Drawing in the mixture from the sides, combine the
dough. Shape into 8 balls and place on the casserole.
Cover and cook for the last 30 minutes.
Serves 4-6

Irish Stew with a Roasted Dumpling Topping

3 LARGE ONIONS, SLICED

1 KG/2 LB BEST END OF NECK LAMB CHOPS, TRIMMED OF EXCESS FAT

3-4 LARGE POTATOES, SLICED

300 ML/½ PINT BEEF STOCK

SALT AND FRESHLY GROUND BLACK PEPPER

FOR THE TOPPING:

125 G/4 OZ SELF-RAISING FLOUR

A PINCH OF SALT

25 G/1 OZ BUTTER

1 EGG

125 ML/4 FL OZ MILK

1 TABLESPOON CHOPPED PARSLEY

1 Arrange a layer of onions in a casserole and put the chops on top.
Mix the remaining onions and potatoes and add to the casserole,
seasoning well. Pour over the stock.

2 Cover the casserole and cook in a preheated oven at 180°C (350°F)
Gas Mark 4 for 1½ hours or until the meat is tender.

3 Make the topping, sift the flour and salt into a bowl and rub in the
butter. Beat the egg and milk and add to the flour mixture with
parsley, stir to form a soft dough. Place the mixture on top
of the casserole and cook for the last 30 minutes or until
the topping is golden brown.

Serves 4

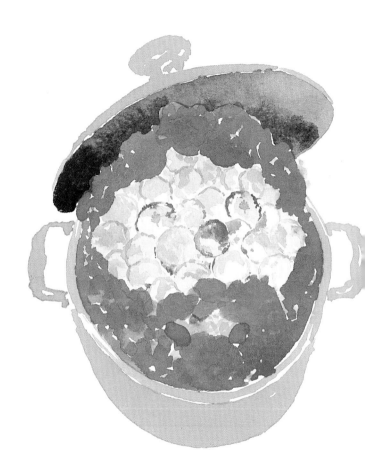

Irish Stew with Pastry Puffs

50 G/2 OZ PLAIN FLOUR

1 ½ LEVEL TEASPOONS SALT

½ LEVEL TEASPOON PEPPER

1 KG/2 LB MIDDLE NECK OR SCRAG END OF LAMB CHOPS

2 ONIONS, SLICED

¾ KG/1½ LBS POTATOES, THINLY SLICED

1 x 250 G/8 OZ PACKET FROZEN PUFF PASTRY, THAWED

1 EGG, BEATEN

CHOPPED FRESH PARSLEY, TO GARNISH

1 Sift the flour, salt and pepper into a bowl. Trim the chops and coat them with the seasoned flour. Put one-third of the onions in a casserole and cover with half the chops. Make a layer with the second third of the onions, then add the remaining chops and top with the remaining onion. Add enough cold water to cover the onions.

2 To make the pastry puffs, roll out the pastry to a 25 cm/10 inch square and cut out 15 rounds with a 5 cm/2 inch fluted cutter.

3 Cover the casserole and bake in a preheated oven at 170°C (325°F) Gas Mark 3 for 1¼ hours. Remove from the oven. Cover the stew with the potatoes and the pastry puffs around the edge of the dish and brush with egg. Cook, uncovered, for a further 45 minutes. Garnish with parsley.

Serves 4

Irish Stew with Beef

A delicious variation on the traditional Irish stew recipe.

50 G/2 OZ DRIPPING
750 G-1 KG/1½-2 LBS STEWING STEAK, CUT INTO
2.5 CM/1 INCH CUBES
350 G/12 OZ ONIONS, SLICED
50 G/2 OZ PLAIN FLOUR
750 ML/1¼ PINTS BEEF STOCK
2 TABLESPOONS TOMATO PURÉE
1 TABLESPOON WORCESTERSHIRE SAUCE
1 TABLESPOON WINE VINEGAR
350 G/12 OZ CARROTS, SLICED
SALT AND FRESHLY GROUND BLACK PEPPER

1 Heat the dripping in a casserole. Add the steak and fry until sealed. Remove and reserve. Add the onions to the dripping remaining in the casserole and fry until golden. Sprinkle in the flour and cook, stirring for 1 minute.

2 Remove from the heat and blend in the stock, tomato purée, Worcestershire sauce and vinegar. Return to the heat, bring to the boil and simmer for 1 minute, stirring. Add the meat and carrots and stir. Cover and cook in a preheated oven at 160°C (325°F) Gas Mark 3 for 2½ hours.

Serves 4

Irish Stew with Butter Beans

1 KG/2 LB MIDDLE NECK OF LAMB, CUT INTO SLICES

1 LARGE ONION, CUT INTO RINGS

2 TEASPOONS MIXED DRIED HERBS

425 G/14 OZ CAN OF BUTTER BEANS, DRAINED

4 LARGE POTATOES, PEELED AND CUBED

300 ML/½ PINT STOCK OR WATER

SALT AND FRESHLY GROUND BLACK PEPPER

CHOPPED FRESH PARSLEY, TO GARNISH

1 Place the lamb slices in a large casserole dish and put the onion rings on top. Sprinkle over the mixed herbs and season well with salt and pepper to taste.

2 Mix the butter beans and the cubed potatoes together and add to the casserole with the stock or water.

3 Cover the casserole and cook in a preheated oven at 180°C (350°F) Gas Mark 4 for 1¼ hours.

4 Sprinkle with freshly chopped parsley and serve immediately.

Serves 4

Lamb Casserole with Chickpeas

2 MEDIUM ONIONS, THINLY SLICED

1 TABLESPOON OLIVE OIL

1 GARLIC CLOVE, CRUSHED

500 G/1 LB LEAN LAMB, CUT INTO SMALL CUBES

1 x 425 G/15 OZ CAN CHICKPEAS, RINSED AND DRAINED

400 ML/14 FL OZ CHICKEN STOCK

1 TEASPOON SAFFRON STRANDS, SOAKED IN 2 TABLESPOONS
BOILING WATER

SALT AND FRESHLY GROUND BLACK PEPPER

2 TABLESPOONS NATURAL YOGURT, TO SERVE

1 Fry the onions gently in the oil in a non-stick pan for 3 minutes; add the garlic and lamb and cook until the meat is evenly coloured on all sides.

2 Transfer the lamb and onions to a casserole and add half the drained chickpeas. Put the remaining chickpeas into a liquidizer or a food processor with the chicken stock, strained saffron liquid, and salt and pepper to taste and blend until smooth.

3 Pour the blended sauce into the casserole. Cover and cook in a preheated oven at 180°C (350°F) Gas Mark 4, or until the lamb is tender. Swirl the yogurt over the top and serve immediately.

Serves 4

Irish Stew with Stout

2 LARGE ONIONS, SLICED

1 KG/2 LB SCRAG END OF NECK OF LAMB, CUT INTO SLICES

2 TEASPOONS MIXED DRIED HERBS

3 LARGE POTATOES, SLICED

300 ML/½ PINT STOCK OR WATER

300 ML/½ PINT STOUT

SALT AND FRESHLY GROUND BLACK PEPPER

1 TEASPOON FINELY CHOPPED FRESH PARSLEY, TO GARNISH

1 Place a third to a half of the onions in a large casserole dish and put the lamb on top. Sprinkle in the mixed herbs and season well with salt and pepper.

2 Mix the remaining onions and sliced potatoes and add to the casserole, seasoning well. Pour over the stock and the stout.

3 Cover the casserole and cook in a preheated oven, at 180°C (350°F) Gas Mark 4 for 1¼ hours. Remove the lid and cook for a further 15 minutes allowing the top to brown slightly.

4 Sprinkle the Irish stew with finely chopped parsley and serve accompanied by colourful vegetables such as peas and carrots.

Serves 4

Irish Stew with Wine and Herbs

1 KG/2 LB BONELESS LAMB, CUT FROM LEG OR SHOULDER

2 TABLESPOONS OIL

250 G/8 OZ BACON, DICED

1 ONION, SLICED

2 CLOVES GARLIC, CRUSHED

1 TEASPOON CHOPPED FRESH MARJORAM

1 TEASPOON CHOPPED FRESH ROSEMARY

120 ML/4 FL OZ RED WINE

2 TABLESPOONS TOMATO PURÉE

SALT AND PEPPER

1 Trim excess fat from the lamb and cut into bite-size pieces. Heat the oil in a frying pan. Add the bacon, onion and garlic and sauté until golden. Remove and set aside.

2 Add half the meat and brown on all sides, then remove from the pan and brown the remaining meat. Return all the meat to the pan with marjoram and rosemary. Season well.

3 Stir in all but 2 tablespoons of the wine and cook until the wine reduces to half of its original quantity. Add the bacon mixture, tomato purée and enough water to cover the meat.

4 Cover and simmer for 1½ hours or until tender. Add the reserved wine just before serving for extra flavour.

Serves 4-6

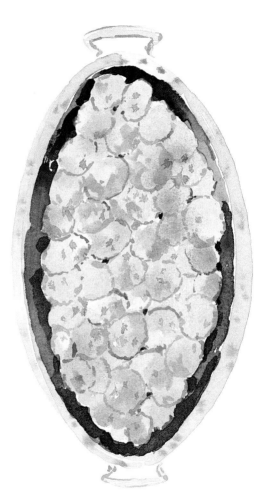

Herby Irish Stew

This stew should taste creamy and fresh, with a subtle flavour of herbs.

1.5-1.75 KG/3¼-4 LBS LEAN NECK OF LAMB, BONED AND TRIMMED

500 G/1 LB ONIONS, SLICED

1 KG/2 LB POTATOES, SLICED

1 TABLESPOON CHOPPED PARSLEY

1 TABLESPOON CHOPPED MARJORAM

A PINCH OF DRIED THYME

600 ML/1 PINT BEEF STOCK

SALT AND FRESHLY GROUND BLACK PEPPER

CHOPPED PARRSLEY, TO GARNISH

1 Cut the lamb into fairly large pieces.

2 Layer the meat in an ovenproof dish with the onions and potatoes, seasoning each layer very well, adding the parsley, marjoram and thyme. End with a layer of potatoes.

3 Pour in the stock, cover with a piece of buttered foil and a tight-fitting lid and cook in a preheated oven at 160°C (325°F) Gas Mark 3 for about 2 hours or until the lamb is tender. If the stew looks dry towards the end of the cooking time, add a little extra stock. Serve garnished with chopped parsley.

Serves 4

Country Irish Stew

750 g/1½ lb best end of neck of lamb, trimmed of excess fat
250 g/8 oz carrots, diced
250 g/8 oz turnips, diced
250 g/8 oz mushrooms
75 g/3 oz pearl barley
1.2 litres/2 pints lamb or beef stock
2 tablespoons tomato purée
1 bouquet garni
250 g/8 oz fresh shelled peas or 125 g/4 oz frozen peas
salt and freshly ground black pepper

1 Fry the lamb in a large flameproof casserole dish until golden, turning once. Take the lamb out of the casserole dish and remove the meat from the bones and then cut into small dice.
2 Return the dice to the casserole. Stir in the carrots, turnips, onions, pearl barley and stock. Add the tomato purée, bouquet garni, salt and pepper to taste and bring to the boil. Cover and simmer very gently for about 50 minutes or until the lamb is tender.
3 Remove the bouquet garni, add the peas and simmer for a further 10 minutes. Skim off any surface fat, adjust the seasoning and serve hot with Irish Soda Bread.

Serves 4

Northern Irish Stew

*In Northern Ireland, Irish Stew is sometimes
made with pork spare ribs. Try this recipe for an unusual
variation on the traditional theme.*

1 25 KG/2½ LBS PORK SPARE RIB CHOPS
SALT
2 LARGE ONIONS, SLICED
1 KG/2 LB POTATOES, SLICED
300 ML/½ PINT CHICKEN STOCK
1 TEASPOON FRESHLY CHOPPED SAGE
SALT AND FRESHLY GROUND BLACK PEPPER

1 Sprinkle the pork with salt and place a layer in a casserole dish.
Cover with a layer of onions and then potatoes. Repeat until
all the onions and potatoes are used.

2 Pour in the stock, sage and season to taste. Cover the casserole
dish and place in a preheated oven at 190°C (375°F) Gas Mark 5
and cook for 1½ hours or until the meat is tender.

3 Serve hot with seasonal vegetables and mushroom ketchup.

Serves 4

Kerry Irish Stew

2 TABLESPOONS OIL

500 G/1 LB POTATOES, THINLY SLICED

750-1 KG/1½-2 LB MIDDLE OR SCRAG END NECK OF LAMB

3 ONIONS, THINLY SLICED

900 ML/1½ PINTS WATER OR LAMB STOCK

SALT AND FRESHLY GROUND BLACK PEPPER

CHOPPED PARSLEY, TO GARNISH

1 Heat the oil in a large saucepan and brown the sliced potatoes. Remove the potatoes and reserve.

2 Cut the lamb into neat joints, then layer the meat, onions and potatoes in the saucepan, seasoning each layer well. Pour over the stock and bring the stew slowly to the boil. Reduce the heat, cover with a lid and simmer gently for 2 hours or until the meat is cooked.

3 Garnish the stew with parsley and serve with seasonal vegetables.

Serves 4

Tipperary Stew

OIL, TO FRY

750 G/1½ LBS STEWING STEAK, CUBED

2 TABLESPOONS PEARL BARLEY

900 ML/1½ PINTS STOCK

250 G/8 OZ ONIONS, FINELY CHOPPED

250 G/8 OZ LEEKS, FINELY CHOPPED

2 STICKS CELERY, CHOPPED

1 MEDIUM PARSNIP, FINELY DICED

1 MEDIUM CARROT, FINELY DICED

1 KG/2 LBS POTATOES, SLICED

1 BAY LEAF

SALT AND FRESHLY GROUND BLACK PEPPER

1 Heat a little of the oil in a frying pan and brown the meat. Transfer to a large flameproof casserole dish, add the barley, stock and seasoning to taste. Bring to a simmer, cover and cook gently for 30 minutes.

2 Add all the other ingredients except the parsley. Mix well, bring to the boil, cover and simmer very slowly on top of the stove, without stirring, for 1¼ hours.

3 Remove the bay leaf before serving.

Serves 4

Connemara Stew

2 KG/4 LBS POTATOES, SLICED
1 KG/2 LB KID OR MUTTON
500 G/1 LB ONIONS, THICKLY SLICED
300 ML/½ PINT WATER
1 BOUQUET GARNI
2 BAY LEAVES
SALT AND FRESHLY GROUND BLACK PEPPER
CHOPPED FRESH PARSLEY, TO GARNISH

1 Put the sliced potatoes into a deep saucepan, add the meat and then all the other ingredients.

2 Cover tightly and simmer gently for 2-2½ hours. Shake the saucepan from time to time to prevent the stew from sticking to the base of the pan.

3 This stew should not be thin. It should be thick, well seasoned and creamy. Remove the bouquet garni and bay leaves before serving and garnish with chopped parsley.

Serves 6-8

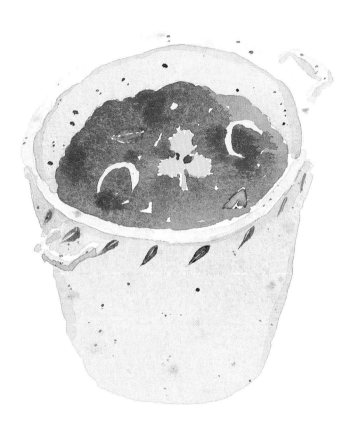

Galway Stew

1 KG/2¼ LBS POTATOES, SLICED

1.5 KG/3 ½ LBS BEST END OF NECK LAMB CHOPS, TRIMMED
OF EXCESS FAT

500 G/1 LB ONIONS, SLICED

4 LEEKS, WHITE PART ONLY, SLICED

2 TABLESPOONS CHOPPED FRESH PARSLEY

1 TEASPOON DRIED THYME

450 ML/¾ PINT CHICKEN STOCK

1 TABLESPOON TOMATO PURÉE

SALT AND FRESHLY GROUND BLACK PEPPER

1 In a large casserole, make layers of potatoes, lamb chops, onions and
leeks, seasoning to taste and sprinkling parsley between each layer.
Begin and end with a layer of potatoes, overlapping the potato
slices in neat rings to form the 'crust'.

2 Mix together the stock and tomato purée and pour into the
casserole. Cover the dish with a layer of foil and the lid.

3 Cook in a preheated oven at 140°C (275°F) Gas Mark 1 for
2 hours. Remove the foil and the lid and add a little more
stock or water, if needed.

4 Return the dish to the oven, uncovered and cook for a further hour,
to brown the potatoes. Serve the stew with seasonal vegetables.

Serves 4

Dublin Stew

This recipe is for beef but you can use lamb.

2 TABLESPOONS OIL

4 LARGE POTATOES, SLICED

750 G/1½ LBS STEWING STEAK

4 ONIONS, THINLY SLICED

300 ML/½ PINT STOCK

SALT AND PEPPER

CHOPPED PARSLEY, TO GARNISH

1 Heat the oil in a large saucepan and brown the sliced potatoes. Remove the potatoes and reserve.

2 Cut the stewing steak into neat cubes, then layer the meat, onion and potato in the saucepan, seasoning each layer well. Pour over the stock and bring the stew slowly to the boil. Reduce the heat, cover with a lid and simmer gently for 2 hours or until the meat is cooked.

3 Garnish the stew with parsley and serve with fresh vegetables such as peas and carrots.

Serves 4

Colonial Irish Stew

A colonial variation of Ireland's most famous stew – from an Irish cook who lives in East Africa.

1 KG/2 LBS LAMB CHOPS
500 G/1 LB SMALL ONIONS, SLICED
1 KG/2 LBS SMALL NEW POTATOES, PEELED
1 CUP OF MILK
SALT AND FRESHLY GROUND BLACK PEPPER

1 Place the loin chops in a large casserole dish,
and cover with warm water.
2 Layer the onions and potatoes over the meat,
and add seasoning to taste.
3 Cover and cook in a preheated oven at 160°C (325°F)
Gas Mark 3 for about 2 hours or until the chops are tender.
4 Remove from the oven, add the milk and serve at once without
reheating, otherwise the milk will curdle.
Serves 4

Braised Red Cabbage

1 SMALL RED CABBAGE, ABOUT 1 KG/2 LBS
1 LARGE ONION, PEELED AND SLICED
2 COOKING APPLES, PEELED, CORED AND SLICED
2 TABLESPOONS SOFT BROWN SUGAR
5 TABLESPOONS WINE VINEGAR
1 BAY LEAF
3-4 TABLESPOONS REDCURRANT JELLY
SALT AND FRESHLY GROUND BLACK PEPPER
CHOPPED PARSLEY, TO GARNISH

1 Finely shred the red cabbage, discarding the stalk and coarse outer leaves. Arrange it in layers in a deep casserole dish with the onion, reserving a few slices for the garnish, and the apples, seasoning well between each layer with salt, pepper and sugar.

2 Pour in the vinegar and tuck the bay leaf down the side of the casserole. Cover closely with a lid or foil and cook in the centre of a preheated oven 150°C (300°F) Gas Mark 2 for 2-2½ hours or until the cabbage is soft and tender.

3 Adjust the seasoning if necessary, stir in the redcurrant jelly and return to the oven for a further 5-10 minutes or until heated through.

4 Garnish with onion rings and chopped parsley.

Serves 4

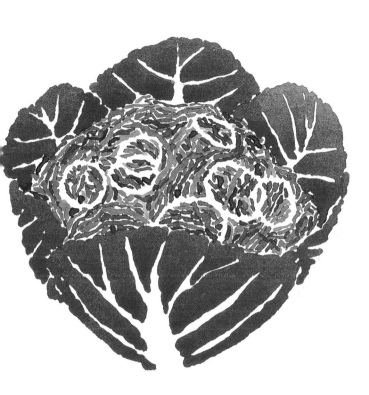

Mushroom Ketchup

*Use the larger flat field mushrooms, preferably when they are
24-48 hours old. This recipe produces a delicious, runny sauce.*

750 G/1½ LBS MUSHROOMS

50 G/2 OZ SALT

300 ML/½ PINT VINEGAR

1 TEASPOON PEPPERCORNS

½ TEASPOON GROUND ALLSPICE

LARGE PINCH EACH OF GROUND MACE,
GINGER, CLOVES AND CINNAMON

1 Wipe the mushrooms, if necessary, and peel them. Break into small
pieces, place in a bowl and sprinkle with the salt. Leave for
abour 12 hours, then rinse and drain.

2 Mash well with a wooden spoon, place in a pan and add the vinegar
and spices. Bring to the boil, then cover and simmer for 30 minutes.
Strain through a sieve.

3 Pour the ketchup into hot bottles and seal.

4 This ketchup must be sterilized immediately. Place the bottles in a
pan of hot water with a false bottom. Bring the water to simmering
point, and simmer for 30 minutes.

Makes approximately 900 ml/1½ pints

Index

Weights and Measures

In this book, both metric and Imperial measures are used.
When working from the recipes, follow one set of measures only,
and not a mixture of both, as they are not interchangeable.

Notes for American and Australian Users

In America, the 8 fl oz measuring cup is used. In Australia, metric
measures are used in conjunction with the standard 250 ml measuring
cup. The Imperial pint, used in Britain and Australia, is 20 fl oz,
while the American pint is 16 fl oz.

The British standard tablespoon, which has been used throughout this
book, holds 17.7 ml, the American 14.2 ml, and the Australian 20 ml.
A teaspoon holds approximately 5 ml in all three countries.

British	American	Australian
1 teaspoon	1 teaspoon	1 teaspoon
1 tablespoons	1 tablespoon	1 tablespoon
2 tablespoons	3 tablespoons	2 tablespoons
3½ tablespoons	4 tablespoons	3 tablespoons
4 tablespoons	5 tablespoons	3½ tablespoons

An Imperial/American Guide to Solid and Liquid Measures

Imperial	American	Imperial	American
Solid Measures		*Liquid Measures*	
1 lb butter	2 cups	¼ pint	⅔ cup
1 lb flour	4 cups	½ pint	1¼ cups
1 lb granulated		¾ pint	2 cups
sugar or caster		1 pint	2½ cups
sugar	2 cups	1½ pints	3¾ cups
1 lb icing sugar	3 cups	2 pints	5 cups
8 oz rice	1 cup		(2½ pints)